BOOK
MEANS
BUSINESS

*Save Time, Make Money,
and Dominate Your Industry
with the Power of a Bespoke Book*

HONORÉE CORDER
with **KENT SANDERS**

YOUR

BOOK

MEANS

BUSINESS

HONORÉE CORDER

and KENT SANDERS

YOUR BOOK MEANS BUSINESS

*Save Time, Make Money,
and Dominate Your Industry
with the Power of a Bespoke Book*

HONORÉE CORDER
with **KENT SANDERS**

E-book ISBN: 978-1-947665-48-4
Paperback ISBN: 978-1-947665-48-4
Hardcover ISBN: 978-1-947665-47-7

ALSO BY HONORÉE CORDER

THE *YOU MUST* BOOK BUSINESS SERIES

- *You Must Write a Book: Boost Your Brand, Get More Business, and Become the Go-To Expert* & *I Must Write My Book: The Companion Workbook to You Must Write a Book*
- *You Must Market Your Book: Increase Your Impact, Sell More Books, and Make More Money* & *I Must Market My Book: The Companion Workbook to You Must Market Your Book*
- *You Must Monetize Your Book: Create Multiple Streams of Income, Diversify Your Earnings, and Multiply Your Impact*

OTHER WRITING BOOKS

- *There is No Such Thing as Writer's Block*
- *Write Your First Nonfiction Book: A Primer for Aspiring Authors*
- *The Bestselling Book Formula: Write a Book that Will Make You a Fortune* & *The Bestselling Book Formula Journal*
- The *Like a Boss* Book Series
- *The Miracle Morning for Writers* with Hal Elrod & Steve Scott
- *The Prosperity for Writers* Book Series

OTHER BOOKS & SERIES

- *Business Networking*
- *Honorée Corder's Mini Book of Goal Achievement*
- *Stop Trying So F*cking Hard: Live Authentically, Design a Life You Love, and Be Happy (Finally)*
- *Tall Order!: Organize Your Life and Double Your Success in Half the Time*
- *The Divorced Phoenix: Rising from the Ashes of a Broken Marriage*
- *If Divorce Is a Game, These Are the Rules: 8 Rules for Thriving Before, During and After Divorce*
- *The Miracle Morning* Book Series with Hal Elrod
- *The Successful Single Mom* Book Series
- *Business Networking: Become a Rainmaker by Building Fantastic Relationships That Stand the Test of Time*
- *Vision to Reality: How Short-Term Massive Action Equals Long-Term Maximum Results*

SPECIAL INVITATION

Watch an informative conversation
with Honorée Corder and Kent Sanders
about the bespoke book process:

HonoreeCorder.com/Interview

This book is dedicated to aspiring authors everywhere. May you experience, firsthand, the magic of being an author.

TABLE OF CONTENTS

PART TWO
CRAFTING YOUR MASTERPIECE

PART THREE
MAXIMIZING YOUR IMPACT

INTRODUCTION

Hello!

I appreciate that your time is more than precious, but I assure you that the time you spend with me throughout this short book can result in a savings of hundreds of hours of work for you. And that's only the beginning.

My goal for our time together is to show you the power of a bespoke book and to help you understand the easiest, fastest, and best path of going from "It would be great if I had a book" to holding your book in your hands and handing it to your next prospect.

You are likely one of the millions of people who would like to have written a book. You may even understand some of the power and leverage authorship can lend to your business. But the truth of the matter is that writing a book is actually difficult. Many of us think we could do it if we only had the time (and perhaps that's true!), but that time can be exceptionally difficult to come by in the midst of your successful and full professional life.

There are many reasons why business leaders miss out on the huge opportunities a book can give them.

They typically fall into one of two categories.

The first category is people who run a successful business but don't have a book.

These people have processes, knowledge, or systems that could help thousands of people improve their lives or businesses. But they haven't put their wisdom into a format that's easily digestible. They're missing out on the huge opportunities that lie on the other side of being an author.

Of course, there's good reason for that! These people likely don't quite understand the value of authorship, and the way that their book can serve their business. Beyond that, they are busy. They have pressing and urgent concerns, and writing a book rarely feels like it is pressing and urgent.

And as I mentioned before, writing a book is actually difficult. Many a seasoned and intelligent professional has tried and failed to successfully complete their book.

The second category is people who *do* have a book, but they don't use it to its full advantage.

Their book probably contains helpful ideas and information. However, it likely hasn't been planned, optimized, or marketed to fully reap the benefits of all that wisdom. These people could be using their book to connect with more customers or clients, boost their credibility, and get more sales.

In either case, the business leader is missing out on a fantastic opportunity to grow their business with a book. Specifically a *bespoke* book.

You, however, are a different kind of leader. You've demonstrated that just by your willingness to spend this short time with me, exploring this topic.

You likely have a suspicion that there's so much more you could be doing if you had a book to help grow your business. I'm thrilled to tell you those suspicions are correct. In the coming pages I'll illustrate exactly why this is true.

But first, I really want to help those of you who are holding out for "someday"—a time in the undefined future—when you will maybe take a sabbatical to finally write your book, those of you who believe that you are the only person who can write your book … I want you to understand the reality of your aspirations.

The hard truth of the matter is this: to write a book that will actually help your business, you must learn essentially an entirely new set of skills and an entirely new business. I want you to shift your mindset and encourage you to think of your book as a marketing asset. Like any other marketing asset, you can try to do it yourself, but your best bet is to hire a professional to get it done right the first time.

In order to understand a little bit more about the bespoke book experience I offer, let's look at another industry that uses a highly "tailored" experience (pun intended!) to make their clients look and feel fantastic.

A TRULY CUSTOMIZED EXPERIENCE

London is a world-class city known for many things: Buckingham Palace, the British Museum, the West End theater district, and the iconic Big Ben clock tower, just to name a few. And who can forget afternoon tea, and fish and chips?

Historical landmarks and beloved cuisine are not the only hallmarks of legendary British culture. For nearly two hundred years, Savile Row has been home to the world's most prestigious tailors.

These custom clothiers, such as Henry Poole & Co., Anderson & Sheppard, and Huntsman (featured in the *Kingsman* films), create suits by hand to each client's exact specifications.

These, and other Savile Row tailors, have created suits and garments for people like Cary Grant, Winston Churchill, King Charles III, Eric Clapton, Al Pacino, and David Bowie.

But they don't just create bespoke garments for men. These tailors have also crafted exquisite clothing for cultural icons like Naomi Campbell, Princess Diana, and Katherine Hepburn, among others.

The term "bespoke" originally referred to clothing that was "spoken for," or reserved for a particular client. Today the term refers to more than high-end custom clothing. It also means any high-quality product that's specifically created for someone to help them feel empowered and more successful.

Savile Row tailors often talk about their clients' emotions when they try on the completed suit or garment for the first time.

They say their clients stand a little taller with pride. The suit has given them more confidence and authority.

They say that "clothes make the man (or woman)." Why? Because the right garment will give you confidence and a boldness you didn't have before. It can open doors and help you show up in the world in a new way.

In other words, bespoke clothing can make a big difference in your business!

But just wait until you see what a *bespoke book* can do.

COULD A BESPOKE BOOK HELP YOU?

Having a bespoke book is an incredibly powerful way to communicate your message to the world and grow your business. But I need to be honest with you: this type of custom book is not for everyone.

It's for the business professional who understands the power of not just having a book but having a *great book*.

It may sound crazy, but not every business leader, owner, or entrepreneur believes they can grow their business with a book. They believe "you can't make money with a book" or "the only way to get a return on my investment is with book royalties."

Furthermore, many business leaders don't invest in creating a great resource (like a bespoke book) to take them further, faster, because they don't know where to start. Also, because no one has helped them see all the possibilities that come from an incredible book, when they do publish a book, they unknowingly cut corners and end up with an inferior product.

I'm here to completely dispel both of these notions in *this* book because I'm living proof that you *can* build a highly profitable business with a great book— and I'm far from the only person who has done so!

Which brings us to the question of who, exactly, would benefit most from a bespoke book.

The clients I work with come in all shapes and sizes, from all backgrounds and types of business. But the quality most of them share is that they want to have a revenue-generating business asset in the form of a book. They see the big picture and understand what having a bespoke book can do for them and their businesses.

Sometimes when I talk to prospective clients, they are focused on earning back their investment through book royalties. Don't get me wrong—I have made plenty of income from book royalties over the past few decades.

But focusing on the royalties is a bit short-sighted. The truth is, the author of a well-crafted book can expect a high return on their investment from more client engagement, at higher fees, more often. Or, they'll sell more products or services, more often (and yes, at higher prices). Book royalties most often come in last.

You *can* make lots of money in royalties. But generally speaking, business professionals who use a book in their business are doing so to generate income from selling products and services, delivering keynote speeches, offering consulting, providing coaching, and many other forms of creating income.

My best advice is to invest in a high-quality book that has evergreen content, one that will work hard to grow your business in the years to come.

WHAT IF I'M LAUNCHING A PRODUCT OR SERVICE?

Sometimes I work with people who are getting ready to launch a new service. Or maybe they have been in the corporate world for years and have transitioned to being an entrepreneur.

You don't need to be established in your current business for years in order to benefit from a bespoke book.

I have crafted books for people who have recently started a new business. They have expertise, a process, or a framework that would benefit their ideal customer or client, and having a book accelerates their progress and compresses the time to profitability.

It's immensely helpful for them to have a book that explains their product or system, and then helps someone get to know them in a way that brings them closer to engagement.

What if, instead of having a whole series of conversations with prospects explaining every aspect of what you do in detail, you could simply give them your book? This incredible resource would do the heavy lifting of providing an overview and answering frequently asked questions, while simultaneously building the relationship. Not only does this approach close the sales loop much faster, but having a book to gift them sets you apart from your competitors. Your book becomes a powerful tool that showcases your expertise, saves time in the sales process, and gives you a distinct edge in the market.

Something *every* businessperson loves!

Imagine that you're a busy CEO and need to hire a consultant to beef up a specific area of your company. You don't have time to listen to a whole series of sales pitches and have conversations with multiple consultants.

Which individual would you most likely hire—the one with a concise book explaining their process and how it could benefit you ... or the one you need to schedule three Zoom meetings with to discover the same information?

I think I know the answer!

A great book isn't just going to close sales faster. It will also simultaneously develop the author-reader relationship, educate your reader about your process or system, and help the reader get to know you as a person.

This is why, during the book planning process, I always talk about the *job of the book*. A book shouldn't be a collection of random ideas. If you're a business leader, your book needs to work hard on your behalf all day every day to close sales and grow your business.

You wouldn't hire an employee and expect them to just sit around all day, would you? Yet that's how most business leaders treat their books.

I collaborate with authors to strategically craft books that enhance their business goals and outcomes.

BESPOKE IS THE MOST POWERFUL WAY TO SPEAK

Let's talk a bit more about the benefit of a bespoke book and how it can help grow your business. There are three main reasons why bespoke is the way to go.

1. You'll save incalculable time in the process.

The average author spends hundreds of hours planning and writing their book—not to mention the countless hours needed to figure out how to publish it. And then there's marketing the book. If this is your chosen path, that's potentially hundreds of hours you would spend when you could have been investing in growing and running your business (or enjoy spending additional time on your hobbies or with your family and friends).

If you're an entrepreneur running your own business, or a C-suite executive with lots of responsibilities, you probably don't have a minute to spare.

I'd wager you have been thinking about writing a book for a while, but you haven't had the time. I'm not a mind reader, but I've worked with hundreds of people at this level. If there's one commonality, it's that they are *busy*.

Here's the good news: when I craft an incredibly effective bespoke book tailored to your message and needs, it will be done in a fraction of the time you could have done it yourself.

2. You'll have world-class experts working on your behalf.

But it's not just a matter of saving time. It's also an issue of expertise.

Look, I know you operate at a high level. You wouldn't be a successful business leader if you didn't. One of the big reasons you've gotten to where you are is because you understand where to invest your efforts.

You know how to delegate and let the experts do their job. That's what makes great leaders so effective.

When you work with me, your bespoke book is carefully crafted by a small team of top-notch professionals who strategize, plan, write, edit, design, and publish your book.

We focus on the *details of your book* so you can focus on the *details of your business*.

3. You'll have a book that is optimized to grow your business.

If you're looking for a high-quality, custom-made suit, you wouldn't go to a chain department store at the mall and grab one off the rack.

You might try and find that, though the measurements might technically be right, even if you had it altered to fit, it's not going to be the best fit for *you*. The shoulders might be too big, the trousers too long, or the sleeves too short. Furthermore, the fabric isn't going to be of the highest quality. And you may have to settle for a color that's less than flattering.

To meet your needs, the garment needs to be tailored to fit your specific goals from the beginning.

Unfortunately, most authors don't take this approach with their books. They don't know that every detail of the book, including the title, cover, outline, contents, positioning, marketing, and other elements, can be optimized.

Your bespoke book, in every detail, is carefully designed and curated to help grow your business.

I understand this may sound bold. Allow me to explain why I am uniquely qualified to help you create a book that exceeds your highest expectations.

WHO IS HONORÉE CORDER?

You're not just looking for someone to publish your book. You're seeking a partner who lives and breathes the art of turning ideas into bestsellers. That's where I come in.

Over the past two decades, I've been in the trenches, crafting and launching more than sixty-five nonfiction books of my own. We're talking nearly five million copies sold across forty languages. But here's the kicker: I've transformed these books into more than a dozen six- and seven-figure income streams. This isn't just a job for me—it's a passion, an obsession.

I don't just write and publish books. I craft, create, market, and monetize them. And now, I'm here to help you do the same and in a way you might not have even thought to imagine.

Hundreds of authors have already trusted me with their book dreams, benefiting from my books, courses, and bespoke publishing services. But let's be clear: I'm not in the business of "just publishing." That's amateur hour.

You may have heard of services like mine, but I ask you to consider if the results from assembly-line style book building are right for you and your business. Many companies that claim to be like mine hire entry-level staff to work with templated book outlines and cover designs ... they may customize some aspects of the book, but they don't really care if your book is good or not. Furthermore, their staff usually doesn't have the talent to *know* how to create an excellent, custom book. That's where I'm different.

My commitment? It's to craft the right book for you. One with laser-focused content, eye-catching design, and compelling calls to action. Why? Because I want your book to do more than sit on a shelf (or collect dust in a box). I want it circulating continuously so it connects with readers, amplifies your impact, and—yes!—multiplies your income.

When you put your book in my hands, you're not making a choice. You're making an investment in yourself, your business, and your future. It's a decision you'll look back on as a turning point in your career.

These days, there are lots of options for publishing a book.

You can try to get an agent who will pitch your book to a traditional publisher. You can work with a hybrid publisher who will let you still own your book while helping you with publishing and marketing. And as I've mentioned, you can try to write and publish it yourself.

There are many wonderful people working at every level of publishing, no matter what the business model.

But I must be honest and tell you that very, very few of them have written dozens of books, sold millions of copies, or worked with so many custom book clients to help them write, publish, and monetize their books.

I know that authors get enamored with their book being a bestseller.

It might be fun to call yourself a "bestselling author." But you know what's even more fun? Being a *best earning* author! Contrary to popular belief, not all bestselling authors are best earning authors—far from it! Most publishers and authors don't understand how to monetize their books effectively. I do.

My goal is not only to help you craft an amazing book. I want it to be a book that brings you more business, more often, at higher fees, so you can maximize your investment and create more income.

WHAT ONE CLIENT HAD TO SAY

I don't want you to just take my word for it. Listen to the kind of experience Beth Walker had working with us on her book *Buying College Better: Have Complete Confidence in Your School of Choice.*

Read this, then hire Honorée to bring your book to life.

Focus on your expertise and time— your most valuable assets. Let Honorée handle EVERYTHING else. In just six months, your book will be available. Don't wait if the world needs your message!

Honorée will accelerate your results, elevate your book, and collaborate fully with you to make the end product incredible. With 20 years of experience and nearly 500 books published, she knows this landscape better than you do. Your book will outshine 98% of what's out there.

She's a one-stop shop: CEO, CFO, COO, CMO, CIO, and amazing human all in one. Honorée takes complete ownership of your success in a way you have to experience to believe.

I've published three books. Thanks to Honorée, I sell more copies of one book annually than most self-published authors do in a lifetime. Hiring her for my latest book?
Best business and personal decision ever.

Don't overthink this. Hire Honorée. Thank me by sending me your book!

THE ROAD AHEAD

BETH IS ONE of the many clients I've helped to create a book that helps grow their business. I want the same thing for you! That's why I've written this book. Here's a sneak preview of what's in store:

In Part 1, we will begin by **Clarifying Your Vision**.

If you want to be the author of a book that changes lives and grows your business, it won't happen by accident. You'll learn about the power of a bespoke book and why it's vital to get clear on your purpose for the book.

I'll also share some thoughts on when to consider doing a bespoke book. As they say, timing is everything!

In Part 2, the focus is on **Crafting Your Masterpiece**.

I work on your book and oversee a team of world-class professionals who help to create your book. You'll learn what each of them does and why each step in the process is so important.

I have a unique way I approach custom books, and I'll give you a sneak peek into all the ways I'm different from other publishers, consultants, and strategists. You'll also learn about different options for your bespoke book.

In Part 3, I will explain how a book can begin **Maximizing Your Impact**.

You probably already know you can publish your book on Amazon. But that's only the tip of the iceberg. There are *lots* more places to distribute your book and get in front of readers.

You'll learn about the most important ones and why they matter.

I'll also share more about one of the most important elements of our process that sets us apart: our customized Book Marketing Action Plan and other assets that supercharge your marketing.

Then I'll conclude the book with some final thoughts on how your bespoke book can bring you more prosperity and success.

If it sounds like we have a full agenda ahead, you're right!

But the good news is that this book won't take much of your time. Although *Your Book Means Business* packs a punch, I have intentionally kept it short.

I mean it when I say that a book can change your life. I'm living proof that being an author is not only a lot of fun—it can also help you build multiple streams of income and take you and your business places you never thought possible!

You have those same opportunities. That's why I'm excited and honored to have you along for the ride.

We may not be traveling to Savile Row in London for a custom-tailored suit ... but having a bespoke book that builds your business is *always* in fashion.

Turn the page to find out what's possible.

Writing a book had always been a goal of mine, but I knew I needed a seasoned guide to help with the complexity and details of the project—especially something I had never done before. Honorée is an absolute powerhouse. From start to finish, she expertly guided the process with a level of detail that is nothing short of mind-boggling. If you're looking for someone who will ensure your project is handled flawlessly, Honorée is the one to trust.

~Dani Whitestone, cofounder, TurboLaw Software, *The Brilliant Businesswoman*

— PART ONE —

CLARIFYING YOUR VISION

CHAPTER ONE

THE POWER OF
A BESPOKE BOOK

WE'VE ALL BEEN to a Fourth of July celebration where there was a dud or two. What's worse than lighting a firework, expecting a big bang, then experiencing that awkward silence?

Sound a little dramatic? Perhaps. But it's nothing compared with the awkward silence of a book that doesn't sell or generate new business in the way it was intended.

Just like a bottle rocket that sits there without shooting into the sky, a book that hasn't been crafted with excellence and purpose isn't going to give you the BANG you're looking for.

I'm not saying the book won't have value. It just won't have the power of a book that's been designed to grow your business.

This isn't just a thought experiment, though. I've been writing books, coaching business leaders, and creating income streams for a long time. Let me tell you the story of how I took one simple idea and turned it into a seven-figure income stream.

ONE CONCEPT
TO SEVEN FIGURES

IN 2015, A little-known company called Amazon asked me to attend an author media breakfast in New York City with four other authors (Pat Flynn, Guy Kawasaki, James Altucher, and my partner and co-creator of *The Miracle Morning* book series, Hal Elrod).

My most recent book at the time was *The Divorced Phoenix*. As a publishing consultant, executive coach, and corporate trainer, I was psyched at the thought of having the full weight of the 'Zon behind me and my book—except that book was a labor of love, it wasn't representative of my current work.

When I suggested to the team I write a book on my area of expertise, they were pleased and encouraged me to do so. In short order, I penned *You Must Write a Book*, and it sold about 50,000 copies in the first few months.

In these past eight years, that book became the first in a series of three books (including *You Must Market Your Book* and *You Must Monetize Your Book*), two workbooks, three courses ("Publishing PhD," "Book Marketing Mastery," and "Building a Million Dollar Book Business"), and the Empire Builders Mastermind. It also inspired *The Bestselling Book Formula* and *Write Your First Nonfiction Book* along with their companion workbooks and courses—a true "mini" empire within my empire.

Although I've been fortunate to experience lots of success with the *You Must ... Book* series, it's not unique to me. I've helped lots of authors build an incredible business from and around their books.

If you're still with me, I have to believe you are at least intrigued by the idea of a bespoke book. Let me share a little more with you about how a bespoke book will help you.

THE #1 BENEFIT OF A BESPOKE BOOK

I'll put this to you as directly as I can: **A high-quality, custom-crafted book will save you time, conserve your resources, and generate maximum revenue.**

Let me elaborate a bit.

One of the biggest benefits of hiring a great team for your book is that they will save you the costly, avoidable mistakes such as hiring the wrong editor or having an inferior book cover designed.

Think about the last time you tried to figure out a process or learn something new. Remember how challenging and frustrating it was to make a bunch of mistakes before you figured it out?

That's exactly what it's like trying to figure out how to write, publish, and market a book on your own. It's an immensely complicated process that requires years of expertise in several different areas. (And we haven't touched on how to effectively monetize your book yet—that's another benefit with an entirely separate learning curve.)

In fact, this is why the whole traditional publishing industry exists!

Traditional publishers have undeniable strengths when it comes to creating high-quality books. (Whether they are optimized to help sell books is another story for another day. But I digress.)

My guess is that you don't have a few extra decades of time and countless dollars that might allow you to master writing, publishing, and marketing your book. You have important activities on your calendar already, such as running and growing your business (which helps you generate wealth for your family and create the legacy you want to leave).

That's where my team and I come in. We come alongside you with our expertise so you can buy back your time. And we will do it faster and to a higher level than you will be able to do on your own.

You only have a certain number of years on this earth. If you try to craft an amazing book on your own, it's only going to distract you from what you're *really put on this earth to do.*

As I mentioned, there are many people and companies who offer similar services.

If I may toot my own horn ever so gently for a moment, I have a great track record of producing high-quality books that get results. I've done it for me and my clients, hundreds of times over the past dozen years.

Few people can match my combination of speed and quality.

You know what it's like to hire people who aren't top-notch. You waste money and energy trying to fix an inferior product. And half the time, you end up hiring someone else to do it right anyway. Yes, I've had people hire me to fix their books—*after* they've invested tens of thousands of dollars to have it published, only to experience lackluster and truly disappointing results.

Sometimes they simply discover there are ways to maximize the book, and they want a do-over so their book can make an even bigger impact.

I'd hate for you to make any of those mistakes.

Partnering with my team will mean you have a high-quality book, enhanced brand visibility, business growth, and industry recognition as a leading expert in your field.

HOW DO I KNOW THIS WILL WORK FOR ME?

At this point you might be thinking, "Okay, Honorée, I'm intrigued. I get that you've had lots of success with your own books. I know you have helped lots of other business leaders with their books. But how do I know all this will work for *me?*"

Look, I don't have a crystal ball. I can't see the future. I'm not a fortune teller, and I don't play one on TV.

But I can use hindsight to imagine the possibilities and feel confident in saying this: *There is almost no business, no industry, that couldn't be helped by a bespoke book.* My diverse client portfolio spans multiple industries. Here are a few examples:

Medical. Matt Feret's *Prepare for Medicare: The Insider's Guide to Buying Medicare Insurance* has helped countless seniors who needed to navigate this complicated program. It also helped establish Matt as one of the go-to Medicare experts.

You'll also want to check out his follow-up book, *Prepare for Social Security: The Insider's Guide to Maximizing Your Retirement Benefits.*

Legal. Ronnie Deaver is a marketing expert who helps attorneys grow their law firms. *The Elite Business Development System for Law Firms: The Fastest Path to 8-Figure Revenue* is a short book that walks attorneys through his unique (and very profitable!) marketing framework.

Financial. A good number of my clients work in or around finance. For example, Beth Walker's book *Buying College Better: Have Complete Confidence in Your School of Choice* helps parents save loads of money on their child's college tuition.

Wade Torkelson's *Secrets Your Creditors Don't Want You to Know* helps people know their rights and eliminate debt. And Ryan Guth, a wealth manager, uses his book *Permission to Exit: Prepare to Sell Your Business Without Regret* to land high net worth clients.

Entrepreneurial. Ali Hemyari, a successful serial entrepreneur, is the founder of the Hemyari Family of Companies, including Nashville K-9 and a partner in Secure Air Charter. He wanted to write a book for his kids that would also help young entrepreneurs learn his framework for success. His first book, *Discipline: What It Really Takes to Build a Seven-Figure Business*, shares his hard-won wisdom.

Dani Whitestone, founder of the Women's Small Business & Leadership Network, wanted to share her knowledge and serve women. The result was *The Brilliant Businesswoman: Your Guide to Entrepreneurial Success*.

Nonprofits. Jeff Conroy is a leadership coach for nonprofit leaders. He needed a short book to show his prospective clients how he could help them and their organizations. That resulted in a mini-book, *Nonprofit Leadership Success: A Short Guide to Big Results*.

Legacy. I've helped craft intimate memoirs for accomplished business leaders seeking to preserve their life stories. These exclusive works, typically limited to a dozen copies or fewer, serve as cherished heirlooms for future generations. Legacy books capture the essence of individuals (or couples) who have built business empires, ensuring their journeys and wisdom endure for their descendants.

This isn't a complete list of industries or individuals who can benefit from having a book, but it gives you an idea of the scope and breadth of the professionals I help.

I can't promise you success, of course. Why? Because the most important factor in your book's success is *you*.

We can create a fantastic book that is well-written and features a fantastic design. But it's all for naught unless it has the proper foundation.

That's the topic of the next chapter, where we will dive into the *purpose* of your book.

CHAPTER TWO

THE PURPOSE
OF YOUR BOOK

IN THE LAST chapter, I mentioned that every bespoke book I create has a job to do. When I work with a client to create their masterpiece, we spend some time getting clear on what their book needs to accomplish.

You see, a book doesn't exist for its own sake. If a book is to reach its full potential, it needs to exist for a reason other than itself. Every book needs a *purpose*—a.k.a. a job.

One of the most fun parts of the bespoke book creation process is helping someone think about what the purpose of their book might be.

Just like you have a set of fingerprints that are unique to you, your book's purpose is as individual as you are. Sure, the general purpose might be similar to many other business leaders' books—like helping you connect with clients, increase your authority, or grow your business.

Invariably, when we really dig into the *why* behind your *what*, we will discover a vision and purpose that are unique to you.

But there's another layer to this. Your book must also serve a purpose *for the reader*. That's why, in our book planning process, we take great care to identify the job of the book for the author, as well as the job of the book for the reader.

A book is a catalyst to make something happen. But that power can only be set in motion when there is a clear purpose. Most books miss the mark on this, because the usual intention is to *publish a book*, not *craft a book with an intended outcome.*

Let's dig into this concept a bit.

THE PURPOSE OF THE BOOK FOR YOU

When you are considering writing and publishing a book, you must begin with a counterintuitive question: *What's in it for me?*

I say that question is counterintuitive because we have all been taught that a book only exists for readers. We are writing books in order to help people and change lives, correct?

Yes, of course. But it's pretty hard to do that unless you begin the book process with a clear intention on what it's designed to accomplish for you and your business.

Consider the airline safety instruction to secure your own oxygen mask before assisting others. This protocol ensures you remain conscious and capable of helping those around you.

In the same way, you won't be able to help readers for long if you don't properly market and monetize your book. The most successful authors have figured out ways to make a lot of money from their books. If they are profitable, they can help more people.

It's a two-sided coin. Winning as an author and helping your readers win are not mutually exclusive goals.

I don't believe in win-lose scenarios in business. I love it when everyone can win! The best scenario is one where authors win by being profitable and seeing a great return on their investment, and their readers win by getting high-quality books (and hopefully more of them over time!).

As you think about the purpose of *your* book, what's in it for you? Do you want to:

- Generate more name, face, and brand recognition for you?

- Produce more leads, customers, clients, or referrals?

- Increase your authority and credibility within your niche or industry?

- Explain your process or framework more succinctly to prospective clients, saving you tons of time?

- Build the foundation for more products and services?

If so, that's fantastic! A book can help you achieve all of those things, and more.

The key is to get very clear on what you want from the book. Once you have that clarity, my team will work with you to carefully craft your book with those goals in mind.

THE PURPOSE OF THE BOOK FOR YOUR READER

All of that said, it's vital to also consider the goal of the reader when they pick up your book.

I've worked with a lot of bespoke book clients over the years, and I can already imagine one question you might have.

"But Honorée, if the book isn't written yet and readers haven't read it, how in the world do I know what they want from it?"

You might be surprised to learn that you already know what your readers want!

Why? Because the readers for your book are the same people you're already talking to every day. They are your ideal prospects, customers, and clients.

You already know their pain points. You're familiar with the challenges they want to avoid and the obstacles keeping them from being successful. You've had hundreds of conversations about your area of expertise.

That's why you don't have to guess what to put in the book. When we work with you on your bespoke book, we naturally draw out those challenges and obstacles—and more importantly, the solutions present in your system or process—and bake them directly into the book.

As I've mentioned before, your book has a job to do. It doesn't just exist for its own sake. When you work with the right team, it will be designed to help sell what you're offering and to help your prospects realize that *you* are the solution to their problem.

If you've been paying close attention so far, you've probably noticed that *Your Book Means Business* is structured to do exactly this. I've written it to help you understand why my bespoke book services are the answer you've been looking for.

In the same way I hope what you're reading is taking you on a journey that leads to us working together, your bespoke book will take *your* target reader on a journey that will lead them to seeking *you* out as the perfect solution to their problem.

Every reader wants to seek pleasure and avoid pain. That pretty much sums up our human motivation. The things we do day in and day out are often motivated by our subconscious desires to seek pleasure and avoid pain.

When readers find your book, it will serve as a beacon of hope, providing solutions that alleviate their pressing concerns or helping them to avoid new ones. They'll be happy to find the promise of quick relief from their challenges or the joy of achieving their desired outcomes.

Just as you're looking for your book to be a catalyst to bring you more business, you reader wants a catalyst to help them succeed.

I hope what you've read so far is getting you excited about the possibilities! When it comes to all the amazing things a book can do for you and your business, the sky's the limit.

Now that you've learned *what* a bespoke book is, and *why* you should consider investing in one, let's turn our attention to the *when*.

As the Good Book says, "To everything there is a season." Is this the right time for you to consider a bespoke book? Let's find out in the next chapter.

I went to Honorée because I heard she was the best Strategic Book Consultant in the world. She pivoted me away from traditional publishing (more $$$$ for me!), introduced me to a fabulous artist, a world class editor, and even

helped me

get on three major podcasts!

Superb work,

best in the world indeed...

~Phil Hellmuth, 17-time World Series of Poker champion and author of *#POSITIVITY: You Are Always in the Right Place at the Right Time, Poker Brat,* and *Play Poker Like the Pros*

CHAPTER THREE

PERFECT TIMING

SINCE YOU HAVE read this far in the book, I can safely bet that you're intrigued. You probably already see the value in having a great team create a book that can grow your business. And you likely already have some ideas about how a book can help sell your products and services.

When I speak to people about bespoke books—or about any other significant investment, such as coaching or a mastermind—they are often interested. But they wonder, *Is now the right time for me to make this investment?*

Before we go any further in this book, I want to reflect on this question a little more. If one or more of the following ideas resonates with you, now might be a great time to move forward with a bespoke book.

IF YOU WANT TO STAND OUT

As a business leader, your job is to stand out from the crowd. In many ways, that is the *main* thing you need to do. If you can't distinguish yourself from others offering the same products and services, you'll be dead in the water in no time.

When networking to grow your business, you need to leave a positive and memorable impression. Handing out business cards hits differently than handing out your book. You want to be the person others remember long after the event ends. Your book is not just a calling card; it's a powerful credential that elevates you above your competitors and makes a lasting impression.

There are other, more specific times when you want to stand out as well, like when you're transitioning from one career into another. Perhaps you are ready to take the leap from employee to entrepreneur, business owner to speaker, or CEO to consultant. Having a book can help provide a seamless transition.

Or maybe you want to stay in the corporate world, but you are shifting into a new role in your company or industry. A book is a fantastic way to elevate your profile.

Why is a book effective? Because everybody wants to be an author, but very few actually do anything about that goal. It truly does set you apart.

In our world of social media and digital influencers, there's still something magical about being an author. When you have a book, you are telling the world that you take yourself seriously, that you're a leader, and that you're a person worth paying attention to.

You are the authority.

IF YOU KEEP ANSWERING THE SAME QUESTIONS

Sometimes being a business leader feels like being the parent of a toddler. If you've had the pleasure of spending any amount of time with young kids, you know they ask a *lot* of questions. Like, every sixty seconds!

The more your business grows, and the more influence you have, the more people will ask you the same questions over and over and over again.

That's a good thing because you want people to be curious about your story, your process, and how you can help them. If you haven't condensed the most common questions (and your answers) into a book, you're probably spending a lot of unnecessary time answering those questions when you could just point them to your book.

In fact, that was the exact catalyst for writing *Your Book Means Business*. I talk to lots of people about bespoke books, and they ask many of the same questions.

Those questions helped me to structure the chapters you're reading.

You can do the very same thing with *your* book. When you're teaching, helping, mentoring, and coaching, you will do a great service for people by compiling your best wisdom into a convenient package they can quickly read.

And the best part? When you have a well-crafted book that both answers their pressing questions *and* arouses more curiosity, they will follow up with more questions. That's a great time to point them toward your other, more expensive offerings like courses, coaching, masterminds, and more.

IF YOU ARE SPEAKING OR FEATURED IN THE MEDIA

TED and TEDx talks have been all the rage in the business world for some time now. And for good reason—many of them are compelling and have changed the lives of both the audience and the speaker. I've given a TEDx talk myself, and I can tell you that it was a great experience. I'll never forget it.

When you're taking any stage, you definitely need a book.

You Must Write a Book wasn't specifically geared toward speakers, yet it most definitely applies to speakers and those focused on getting more speaking engagements (more often and at higher fees—are you picking up on a theme here?). I personally know of dozens of speakers who have penned books after reading my book, and as a result they were able to increase their speaking fees *and* get booked to speak more often! Books and speaking go hand in hand like peanut butter and chocolate!

The same goes if you're being featured in the media. Maybe there's an article coming out about your business, you're doing a television interview, you're appearing on podcasts, or you're doing radio interviews. Mention the title of your book in your three-sentence bio and your credibility immediately soars.

Anytime you find yourself in front of people, that's a great time to have a book. Why? Because if you have a compelling message, they always want to know more about you. A book is a low-cost, convenient way for them to digest your message and get into your ecosystem.

IF YOU HAVE A STORY TO TELL

Up to this point, I've emphasized that a book is a great way to share your process, framework, or system to your ideal client or customer.

But not every business leader wants to approach their book this way. Sometimes they want to tell their life story or teach certain principles in the form of a story-driven business book.

Maybe you've had people continually tell you some version of this: "You have a great story. You should write a book about it!"

If so, this might be a great time to think about how to best capture that story in the form of a book so that many other people can enjoy it. When you combine a compelling story with speaking, coaching, or masterminds, that's a pretty effective way to not only reach more lives—but also to monetize your message.

IF YOU WANT TO BOOST YOUR BUSINESS

The top-grossing movie of 2022 was *Top Gun: Maverick*. In the opening scene, Maverick (played perfectly by Tom Cruise) pilots the DarkStar, a fictional experimental aircraft. He wants to push its limits to prove it can reach Mach 10.

In order to do this, Maverick has to boost the engine's power by switching to scramjet. Scramjet pushes the plane into new territory by giving it a boost not available with conventional engines.

Don't get me wrong—there are lots of effective ways to grow a business. But time and again, I've seen the extra boost a book can give to a business. A *bespoke* book packs even more power—similar to having a state-of-the-art jet engine.

Nothing can capture your message, solidify your authority, and command attention quite like a book.

NOW IS A GREAT TIME!

Anyone who has been in the business world for even a short time has heard the old Chinese proverb "The best time to plant a tree was twenty years ago. The second-best time is now."

You can't go back in time twenty years to create that book you've always wanted. After all, technologies like Marty McFly's time-traveling DeLorean don't exist *quite* yet.

Who would want to go into the past anyway? The future is much more exciting!

It's a good thing, too, because you *can* change your future—and the future of the people your business serves—with a well-positioned book that's crafted by experts.

In these first few chapters, I've helped you clarify your vision by thinking about the power, purpose, and timing of a bespoke book. I hope you feel more motivated than ever to share your story, process, and wisdom in a book!

If you are, you're probably also wondering how a bespoke book is actually created. You're in luck, because in Part 2 I will lead you through my proprietary process of crafting your book.

I can't wait to introduce you to the team and process that will make it happen, in addition to the options we have for you!

— PART TWO —

CRAFTING YOUR MASTERPIECE

CHAPTER FOUR

YOUR BESPOKE BOOK PUBLISHING TEAM

IN THE INTRODUCTION, I mentioned that my goal for bespoke books is similar to the goal of Savile Row tailors in London. I want to create a highly personalized, amazing experience that rewards you for years to come.

Anyone who knows me will tell you that I'm just a *wee bit* enthusiastic about the power of books! (That may be a bit of an understatement.) I spend most of my workdays planning, writing, strategizing, or monetizing books for me and my clients. And if I'm not doing that, I'm probably meeting with someone or doing a podcast interview about that same topic.

That said, even my boundless energy isn't enough to create an amazing bespoke book all by myself. That's why I have a team of people around me who bring their considerable talents to the table.

When you delegate each aspect of book production to professionals, you have a book that's done *better* and *faster* than if you were to do it yourself.

Savvy, successful leaders and entrepreneurs hire experts for various needs in their business and personal life because they don't have time or energy to do it all themselves (and/or they don't know how!). They know they need a *who*, not a *how*. If there's one other important thing every great leader knows, it's this: you won't get where you want to go all by yourself.

Delegate, don't complicate.

The same is true for creating a great book. It's only going to happen when you engage the talents of an incredible team.

Let's take a look at each of these roles in more detail. This will help you better understand how they will create *your* masterpiece.

EXECUTIVE BOOK PRODUCER

As the strategist and executive book producer, my job is not only to shepherd the project from beginning to end, but to also ensure the author is thinking about the book from all different perspectives.

I want to make sure we get very clear on the job of the book for you as well as the reader. That's a cornerstone to the overall success strategy for a book.

Most publishers put their focus on creating a great book. A lot of great books are not very successful, though, because the publisher and author don't know what to do with them once they're out in the world.

The job of the book must be determined *before* the book is written; in fact, *before* the outline is created, a working title is selected, or a target publication date is set. *It's that important.*

Which is why I personally work very closely with you to identify the *why* for you, the author, and for your reader, but also to keep an eye toward how you'll eventually market your book, as well as market *with* your book.

Successfully launching and marketing a book requires strategic decision-making across multiple areas.

The book's core elements—including its content, bonuses, cover design, interior layout, and sales copy—must be carefully crafted in service of your message and purpose.

Equally crucial are the prelaunch and launch activities, such as assembling an Advance Reader Team (ART), securing endorsements, and initiating a word-of-mouth campaign.

Both short-term and long-term marketing strategies need thorough planning, encompassing elements like the author's website (including the book's landing page), promotional bonuses, and tactics for marketing both the book itself and using it as a tool for broader marketing efforts.

By giving careful thought to each of these components, authors can maximize their book's long-term potential and increase its chances of success in the market.

It's important to understand where the book fits into your business and how will you use it in the future.

I also act as the chief quality control officer. I have a proprietary thirty-seven-point review process I apply to every book to ensure maximum effectiveness and return on the author's investment.

Everyone on my team maintains *very* high standards, as high as the Big 5 New York publishers, in our writing, editorial, and design excellence.

In addition, I oversee the entire team as we move through the book creation process.

My goal is to make your life—and business—easier at every turn of the book creation process. My commitment to you is that I will treat your book as if it were my own, making sure it is absolutely the best it can be.

GHOSTWRITER

I'll talk more about the process of working with a ghostwriter in the next chapter. For now, I want to emphasize that a ghostwriter will write the book better and faster than you could do it on your own.

Why? Because the writer is a professional who knows how to extract your knowledge to create the book's content quickly, craft the compelling stories that will resonate with your readers, and present your knowledge and wisdom in a way that positions you as the expert.

I'm sorry to be the bearer of bad news, but even if you write quite a lot in your chosen profession, the likelihood of you writing a great book out of the gate is … quite low. Ghostwriters are skilled, professional writers with a skillset finely honed to deliver excellent prose in a short time.

Many would-be authors worry that using a ghostwriter is somehow "cheating" or that the writer won't be able to capture their voice.

Using a ghostwriter is actually one of the smartest things you can ever do as a business leader. Why? Because you have better things to do with your time than struggle to find the right thoughts and words and attempt to put them in the most effective order.

Keep in mind that every high-level business person uses writers. Whenever the President gives a speech, he always uses a writer. The stakes are too high for him to try to "figure it out," and the same point must be made for your book.

You probably wouldn't try to fix your car engine or your plumbing by yourself (unless you're good at those tasks). So why would you struggle with the writing? Trust me on this one, and let a pro handle it!

Plus, you've already been using a ghostwriter for years. How so? Every time you buy a greeting card, customize a prewritten email template, or used someone else's thoughts, essentially you've hired another writer to help express your thoughts.

A ghostwriter saves you *loads* of time and energy, which you can spend on more important matters. And ironically, they make you sound more like yourself than you can! How? A great ghostwriter pays attention to how you communicate, listening for frequently used words and phrases. They analyze the vibe, tone, and rhythm of how you speak and then translate that into writing that sounds remarkably like you.

In fact, if you have met me personally or heard me on a podcast, you might have thought that I'd written this book myself. You may have noticed the words *with Kent*

Sanders on the cover. That's publishing speak for "someone other than the author (probably) wrote this book." In order for me to speak authentically about using a ghostwriter, *I literally used a ghostwriter for this book.*

Due to the compact size of the book, it took us just one ninety-minute interview to capture the contents of this book, *and I'm a professional writer!*

I'll leave you with this for now: if you're not a professional book writer, the hours you can save on the first draft alone begin at about fifty and can easily be in the hundreds. Imagine saving potentially a month's worth of time and ending up with a better product.

COPY EDITOR AND PROOFREADER

Every writer needs a highly trained, experienced editor. (At least one.) And a proofreader—probably two! By the time this book is published, it will have been through at least one round of editing and a round of proofreading by a second set of eyes.

Getting to a final first rough draft is one challenge; however, putting the spit and polish on a manuscript and turning it into the book you hold in your hands is quite another. It requires hours of skilled, focused work, all while adhering to a manual of style and high standards, to ensure a smooth read by the reader.

I liken a great editor to a magician. Editors evoke feats with words and inspire improvements that elevate your book to its finest form. They pay attention to things like the way the sentences and paragraphs flow and to the structural narrative of your book so that your reader gets the very best reading experience possible.

The editor's efforts are supported by a proofreader, who makes sure the finished product shines with perfection. A typo—a missing word, a misspelling, a misplaced apostrophe—can make the reader feel like they've hit a speed bump in a Ferrari at full speed. The editorial team double-checks the accuracy of information and corrects inconsistencies.

With a bespoke book, while still independently published, you won't hear the complaints typically made about self-published books: *There were typos on every page!*

(If a typo does get through, and occasionally they do, keep in mind that 100 percent accuracy is nearly impossible considering the number of words versus the persistence of that typo.)

COVER AND INTERIOR DESIGNER

I know we've all heard the mantra: *Don't judge a book by its cover.* But we all do it! You do it, I do it, and it doesn't stop with the book's cover.

For now, let's discuss the fact that your book's cover will ensure one of two things happen when someone sees your book: they will feel compelled to read it or *they won't.*

If your book cover design isn't spot on, if it doesn't fit in with the other books in its genre—and *stand out among them*—because it isn't outstanding and compelling, your book won't stand a chance.

When I published my first book, I made the mistake of using a graphic designer instead of a *book designer*—someone who takes all of the elements of your book (text, illustrations, front and back covers) and puts it together into one harmonious package. The graphic designer made a great-looking image, but it wasn't designed to sell books.

Think of it this way … When you go to buy a dozen bagels at the store, you are expecting to see them arranged on the shelf in clear plastic bags with some kind of product label. If someone were to package their bagels in a pink donut box, even if the label clearly said "bagels," most people in search of bagels wouldn't even *see* the pink box of bagels. Their brain would have already decided the package's contents were donuts.

The very same thing happens with books. A great cover tells the reader far more than "this is a book." A great cover will feel the same as, but different from, other books in its niche. Think back to the "bodice ripper" covers of dime-store paperback romance novels. There is a reason there are so many of them ... They effectively convey to the reader what they will find inside those books.

The designer on my team is a genius who specializes in book cover design. They will ensure your cover delights you enough to take your breath away while doing the job of exciting the reader and working overtime to grow your business.

When you work with my team, your book's cover will be custom made for you—you won't ever see another book with your cover (unless someone steals your design)—and it will be one you share with pride. We don't work with a small selection of cover templates and offer everyone the same cookie-cutter approach.

And it's not just your cover that will get the five-star treatment.

The interior design of your book should harmonize with its cover, incorporating elements that echo throughout the pages. While a simple interior design can suffice, a thoughtfully crafted bespoke design works subtly yet powerfully for you and your business, leaving a lasting impression on readers even at a subconscious level.

To achieve this cohesive and impactful design, both your book's cover and interior should be entrusted to a professional whose expertise lies specifically in book design and formatting. This specialist will bring their creative vision and deep understanding of book aesthetics to ensure your work stands out and resonates with your audience while meeting the standards required by the big publishers so that you don't run into surprise headaches just before publication.

COPYWRITER

Crafting compelling back cover copy is a critical yet often overlooked aspect of book publishing. A skilled copywriter plays a pivotal role in capturing potential readers' attention and persuading them to purchase the book.

This concise text must distill the essence of your work, highlight its unique value, and create an irresistible hook—all within a limited space. An experienced copywriter is a marketing expert who understands how to balance intrigue with information, and uses powerful language to evoke emotion and curiosity. They can effectively communicate your book's core message, hook your target audience, and rapidly define your book's key selling points, ultimately turning browsers into buyers.

My team includes a professional copywriter to significantly enhance your book's marketability and contribute to its overall success in a competitive publishing landscape.

One interesting thing to note: while your cover is the hook that interests a prospective reader (and your future client) to look at the book, the back cover (a.k.a. jacket) copy confirms the book is something that they could be interested in. They may be compelled to read a few paragraphs of the book to sample the writing style. If that also checks the box for them, then the purchase is likely made.

PUBLISHING COORDINATOR

My publishing coordinator is an indispensable member of your book production team, serving as the linchpin for all administrative aspects of the publishing process.

This detail-oriented professional manages a myriad of crucial tasks, ensuring that nothing falls through the cracks. From setting up retail accounts across various platforms to meticulously verifying every piece of information about your book, they leave no stone unturned.

They act as a vigilant guardian of deadlines, coordinating with various team members to keep the project on track. Their expertise in navigating the complex world of publishing logistics means that ISBN registration and distribution setups are handled seamlessly. By managing these essential behind-the-scenes elements, our publishing coordinator ensures your book launches effectively and on schedule. Their role is vital in transforming your manuscript from a personal project into a professionally published work ready for the marketplace.

Because I only use the best in the business for your book—there's that high standard again—it can, and will, sit next to a traditionally published book and shine.

There you have it! Now you have an idea of the main players on my incredible team who will help bring your book to life.

THE REAL COST OF DIY

This is a good opportunity to remind you about the *cost* of trying to do all this by yourself or hiring a team of folks who don't know (really) what they're doing.

When I talk to successful business leaders who want to write and publish a book, I will occasionally run into someone who makes a lot of money in their business, but they balk at the cost of hiring professionals to work on their book.

It's not just a matter of being cheap. Most of the time, they simply don't know what is involved in creating an incredible book. In addition, they don't realize how much it will cost them to DIY this important project; or they will hire people as cheaply as possible—and get what they pay for (which won't be what they really want).

When you release a poorly written and published book into the world, it will cost you in three ways:

1. YOU WILL WASTE HUNDREDS OF HOURS.

The expertise required to strategize, write, and publish a book is significant.

You will spin your wheels and get frustrated because there is a *lot* to learn.

2. YOU WILL LOSE OPPORTUNITIES.

As a business leader, you understand *opportunity costs*. It's those chances to network, plan, dream, execute, and build that you won't have because you were consumed by the details of writing and managing your book yourself.

Further, a poorly published book won't compel anyone to read your book, and if they do, they certainly won't engage you. They'll assume your book is a reflection of how you conduct business.

3. YOU WILL PUT YOUR REPUTATION AT RISK.

Let me be brutally honest for a moment. If you publish a poorly written and designed book, people will not say anything to your face. They will congratulate you and act thrilled that you're an author. But behind closed doors, they will talk amongst themselves about the poor quality of the book you released.

I've seen it happen *many* times. Trust me, you *do not* want to be the person who is known in your peer group (and beyond) for putting your name on a half-baked book.

No business leader would ever knowingly risk doing anything that would cost them hundreds of wasted hours, opportunities to grow their business, and possibly their reputation.

Yet I see it all the time when otherwise successful people try to DIY a book, produce it with an inexperienced team, or publish as cheaply as possible. All in the name of saving a few bucks.

Your book isn't just a product—it's an extension of who you are as a person. It represents your brand, your voice, and your value. Done well, it can serve as an evergreen extension of *you* in your marketplace.

If you think you can't afford a bespoke book, the truth is, you can't afford *not* to invest in one!

Your name and reputation are far too valuable to risk with an inferior book. In the next chapter, we'll dive into the process of how we craft your book so you can see the extent to which my team works on your behalf. Later, we'll talk about how investing in a bespoke book has a huge potential upside.

CHAPTER FIVE

CREATING YOUR
BESPOKE BOOK

BACK IN THE 1990s, when DVDs first came out, movie studios needed a way to entice consumers to switch from VHS to the new format.

Any discerning viewer would immediately notice the advantages of DVDs over VHS. The image was crisper and you never had the problem of a VHS player eating the movie! DVDs were also slimmer and easily portable.

But switching formats meant that customers needed to purchase new equipment, so there was a significant hurdle to overcome.

When trying to figure out how to market DVDs to consumers, studios needed something extra. Aside from the advantages of having a better picture and being more portable, there was another killer feature that made DVDs a no-brainer in comparison to VHS tapes: the *exclusive behind-the-scenes features.* These absolutely helped shift the market to DVDs, and once everyone had a DVD player, bonus content continued to play a role in which DVDs you selected to purchase.

Since streaming services have taken over the world, studios don't seem to bother with these much anymore. But back in the day, you could expect lots of behind-the-scenes features on DVDs, especially if the movie was a big release.

There was a simple reason for this: people *loved* learning about the process of how their favorite movies were made, and they loved being someone *in the know.* When someone asks you for your business card and you hand them your bespoke book, it's like you are giving a DVD to a person who has a stack of unwound VHS tapes. They will experience a bit of a thrill, because you are handing them something tangible, with value … something with exclusive bonus content.

At this point in the book, I hope that you're excited about the possibility of what a bespoke book can do for your business. Now that you've met the types of professionals I employ for your book's production, let's dive into the actual process of how my team creates your bespoke book.

This will help you know what's going on behind the scenes, what to expect, and how long it will take. Best of all, I hope you'll appreciate the carefully designed process that's in place to ensure you have the best bespoke book possible.

AN UNPARALLELED PROCESS

The goal of my exclusive process is very simple. I want to help you unleash your vision and create more than a book—I want to help you craft your legacy.

My unparalleled process delivers:

- A masterfully written manuscript, breathed into life by a skilled ghostwriter
- Prose refined to perfection by a seasoned editorial team
- Visually stunning design that captivates and elevates your work
- Magnetic sales copy and back cover text that compels readers to action
- A tailor-made Book Marketing Action Plan and additional resources strategically designed to catapult you and your book's success

It's all about amplifying your voice and vision. Better yet, you retain full copyright, creative control, and 100 percent of the royalties and income.

We blend the best of traditional publishing, including quality and distribution, with the flexibility and ownership of independent (indie) publishing. As a result, your book can make the impact you want it to—for yourself, your business, and your readers.

With that said, let's take a closer look at each of the steps involved in creating your masterpiece!

STEP 1: STRATEGIC PLANNING SESSION

After you formally engage my team with the signing of a contract and investment in your bespoke book, we schedule what I lovingly refer to as a "kickoff meeting." Just like a football game begins with a kickoff, we start our process with a strategic planning session designed to move the ball—i.e., your book—down the field.

As your publishing strategist, I'll lead an initial meeting with you, your ghostwriter, and other key team members. We begin by clarifying your book's purpose. Is it to generate income, create impact, or achieve another specific goal? I'll guide you through this crucial decision-making process. My team is there primarily so that they can come to thoroughly understand you and your business.

In addition to thinking about the job of the book for *you*, we refine the job of the book for the *reader*. What is the transformative journey your book is designed to accomplish for them?

During this meeting, we also agree to the production schedule for the book. This includes key dates for the book's outline, the first draft, final draft, publishing date, and more.

These dates aren't rigid—we take life (ours and yours) into consideration, as well as holidays, your business travel, summer vacations, and other situations that may arise. The important thing to know is that we have a clear start date and a clear publication date for your book.

This production schedule not only keeps everyone on track, it also gives you confidence that we will deliver your book on time, as well as a deep understanding of the multiple steps we will take to ensure you are happy with the finished product.

As I will elaborate on shortly, *a book in motion is money in motion.* We maintain a careful balance of quality and speed so your high-quality book is delivered on time, every time.

The most important factor impacting the production timeline is the size of the book.

- A 5,000-word book will take approximately ninety days.
- A 15,000- to 20,000-word book will take approximately six months.
- A larger book of 50,000 to 70,000 words or more will take approximately twelve months.

In general, your book's timeline of three, six, or twelve months depends on the size of the book. Your level of urgency also plays a role—if you have a need for your book sooner than later, we can discuss accelerating the timeline for an additional fee. Conversely, your lack of urgency or availability would make the process take longer.

We know that once you're ready to begin the process, you'll want your book finished sooner rather than later. With my team you will always get it quickly, but not before it's ready.

STEP 2: OUTLINE AND WRITING

Once we have a firm plan in place, then we get to work outlining and writing the book. For this section, Kent Sanders (the ghostwriter of this book), explains how the ghostwriting process works.

Hi, Kent Sanders here. I love working with Honorée and her bespoke book clients. Once we have concluded our kickoff meeting with Honorée and everyone is clear on the job of the book for you, the author, as well as your readers, then you and I will get to work developing a preliminary document that includes a detailed book outline. The primary reason we begin here, instead of diving right into writing the book, is to make sure we have a clear structure for the book.

The main purpose of a book outline is to ensure that we're taking your reader on a journey of transformation. What does every great story have in common? The hero goes through some kind of change where they grow, learn, or improve.

We want the same thing for your reader. Generally speaking, your reader wants to have success around the topic of your book. Whether it's weight loss, real estate, getting a better deal on college, exiting their business, or any other topic, the goal is the same: helping the reader be more successful.

In addition to the outline itself, I include a few other items in this preliminary document before we begin writing:

- Ideas for book titles and subtitles.
- The key problem this book solves for the reader.

- Details about the audience and what they want from the book (sometimes called a psychographic profile of the reader).

- Details on what makes this book different from others in the same niche.

We typically have some back and forth as we discuss these items. As a writer, I want to make sure I'm laser-focused on your goals for the book. I also want to understand the audience and the problem we are solving for them.

It usually takes about two weeks to prepare this document and work through it with you. If we're talking about a full-length book of 50,000 words or more, the process will take four to six weeks because the book is more complex.

Once we have a clear vision for where we're going, we can start working on the first draft of the book with certainty and confidence!

During this process, which can take anywhere from a few weeks to nine months, depending on the book size, the book takes shape in several steps:

1. We schedule a series of calls to gather content for the book. I ask lots of questions to prompt your thinking, stories, framework, and other related material I'll use to create your book's first draft. A general rule of thumb is that we need one hour of interview time for every five thousand words of completed book content.

2. I create an outline for you to review. The outline for your book can take one to four weeks, depending on the size of the book. Once completed, we'll meet with Honorée to review the outline and make any strategic adjustments.

3. I create drafts of the chapters for you to review. If it's a shorter book (15,000 words or less), I send you a completed **rough first draft**. If it's a longer book, I break it up into sections, typically delivering a couple of chapters per week. Once the rough draft is completed, we again meet with Honorée. Together, the three of us determine if the content meets your expectations, or if we need to course correct.

4. You add comments and edits to the draft. Although you're working with a ghostwriter, you're still doing some writing and editing to ensure the book meets your vision. We also want to get the details and nuances right when it comes to your topic. Depending on the state of the rough first draft, we may need to add or remove sections of the book, set up another call or two to gather additional material, or make lighter edits.

5. We keep revising until we have a final first draft. This is a draft that is ready for the editor. At this stage, we meet again with Honorée to sign off on this final first draft.

Even though no two books are the same, we keep this proven process remarkably consistent. It has worked extremely well so far, allowing us to get books done quickly and with minimal life disruption to the author.

Now I'll turn the book back over to Honorée!

Thanks, Kent! As you can maybe see, Kent's writing style, his voice, is markedly different from mine. The great thing about using a ghostwriter is they write in your voice, so every word sounds like *you* wrote it (because in essence you did—you just *said them first*). A great ghostwriter has three special skills (a.k.a. superpowers):

- Writing quickly and efficiently
- Capturing the author's voice
- Arranging all of the spoken content into a cohesive, comprehensive manuscript

Underestimating the need to use these superpowers is a mistake, and if you started this book with any reservations about using a ghostwriter, I hope I have given you reason to reconsider. The best ghostwriters seemingly effortlessly create the book you would have written had circumstances allowed.

STEP 3: BOOK STRATEGY

While the ghostwriter is working with you to craft the contents of the book, there is a virtual ballet going on behind the scenes.

Like a duck hanging out on a lake— calm on the surface but paddling like hell beneath—as your team captain, I'll be:

- Coordinating the swift yet brilliant production of your manuscript into a book with my top-tier design and editorial teams.

- Crafting your personalized Book Marketing Action Plan based on our discussions about your business and what you want to happen once you have your book.

- Developing complementary publishing assets to maximize your book's success, which include ways to repurpose the content with your expertise to create additional revenue streams.

- If appropriate, setting up your global distribution channel accounts (including Amazon and others) for worldwide availability, including bookstores, major retailers, and libraries.

- And more. *There's always so much more!*

STEP 4: EDITORIAL

When the final first draft is finished and approved, the book goes to the editorial and proofreading stage.

I work with an experienced editor to ensure the grammar, sentence structure, punctuation, word tense and usage, and other elements are correct. As I mentioned earlier, this sounds like a litany of *boring*, but what they do is absolutely magic.

After that, the book goes to a proofreader, who does another pass. They are checking for those tiny errors that so easily remain in the book (if you see one in here, be sure to let me know—it wasn't for lack of an extensive review process). They also make sure the book adheres to a standard style guide for ease of reading. My goal is for your book to be flawless.

STEP 5: BOOK DESIGN AND DESCRIPTION

After the book has been edited and proofread, it goes to our world-class designer. By this point, concepts for the cover design will have already been underway and I will have shown you some preliminary designs for the cover.

But that's only part of the design process. Many authors focus all of their design attention on the book cover and forget about the interior. The inside of the book is an incredible opportunity to tie in design elements from the cover. By doing so, you'll give the reader an opportunity to engage with your topic through consistent design choices.

The cover design is typically created during the writing process, but the interior layout can only happen once the manuscript is completely finished and approved by you. Small changes in text can have ripple effects throughout the manuscript in terms of formatting, so it's best to start formatting after the final manuscript is ready so we don't spend additional, unnecessary time in the formatting process.

Concurrent with the design process, my copywriter will create a book description designed to sell your book. This description will be featured on the book's back cover, on your website, on retailer websites, and more.

I do want to emphasize that you, as the author, are involved in each of these steps! I continually seek your feedback to ensure the book truly represents your vision.

After all, we aren't just publishing your book—we're creating a powerful, revenue-generating business asset that aligns perfectly with your goals and amplifies your influence.

STEP 6: PROOFS AND PUBLISHING

Once the cover, description, and book interior are finished, our publishing coordinator uploads the book to online retailers, and I follow behind to ensure every detail is perfect. We then order proof copies to review as a final quality check.

I've been in the nonprofit world for over 30 years and always felt I had a book inside me, but I struggled with structure and content. Then I connected with Honorée Corder and her team—Kent Sanders and MJ James—and everything changed. They made it happen.

Every step of the way, they consulted with me, making sure the process was smooth. From the layout to the cover design, to all the tech stuff that connected my book to online bookstores around the world—they handled it all. Honorée and her team were not only knowledgeable but also incredibly friendly and patient with all my questions.

After the book was released, they didn't stop there. They helped spread the word through their network, ensuring it reached as many people as possible. I couldn't have asked for a better team to work with on such a personal project. Thanks to Honorée, MJ, and Kent, not only did I create my first book, but I also gained three new friends!

~Jeff Conroy, *Nonprofit Leadership Success: A Short Guide to Big Results*

A proof is just like the final print version, except it typically has "Not for Resale" or similar language on the cover to indicate it's not the official version. You'll get a copy to admire as well!

As the book strategist, I do a robust, highly detailed quality check of the proof copy to ensure the book is impeccable. My team corrects any lingering errors, and then creates the final files. (Keep in mind, you'll be blissfully unaware of these parts of the process.)

After that, your book is ready for publication and launch!

If you're like most of my clients, you have investigated other options for publishing. The steps I've just described will be familiar to you. Planning, outlining, writing, editing, proofreading, publishing—these are the basic activities of any company serving authors.

So, what sets us apart? What do we do differently, and how do we serve authors at a higher level? That's the topic of the following chapter.

CHAPTER SIX

YOUR PUBLISHING POWERHOUSE

IF YOU SPEND much time around authors, it doesn't take long to hear some talk about publishing options today.

Should you go with a traditional publisher, which usually involves finding an agent first? Should you use a hybrid publisher, which usually lets you keep your royalties but has some functions of a traditional publisher? Or should you go indie and try to figure it all out for yourself?

It can be a challenge to decide the most effective path for authors, even those who have multiple books. If you're never written and published a book before, the options seem endless, and you might not know where to even start.

That's why in this chapter we'll take a quick look at what makes my bespoke publishing experience so different.

In a nutshell, I provide the high quality of traditional publishing, the flexibility and benefits of indie publishing, plus the experience of professionals who have "been there, done that" hundreds of times.

Quality matters to me, as much or more than profitability, because I know my reputation hinges on each and every book that I put my stamp of approval on.

Let's explore the specifics of what sets my service apart a bit more.

WHAT SETS ME APART?

When you work with me and my team, you'll find we are a true publishing powerhouse for several reasons.

1. We craft a high-quality product that rivals the end product of traditional publishers.

One of the biggest complaints about the self-publishing industry is that many indie books are poorly crafted. The writing, cover design, editing, and formatting are often sub-par (and frankly, that's being generous). When you work with my team, however, the final product is a book indistinguishable from those the big New York publishers produce.

We include the tiny details you'd find on any book at Barnes & Noble or Target, such as a flawless read, quality design inside and out, and more.

2. You'll get your book in a fraction of the time traditional and hybrid publishers take.

When you sign with a traditional publisher, there is often a two-year time frame between signing a contract and the book release. Hybrid publishers often take a year to get your book to market. With my team, your bespoke book is done in a fraction of that time.

For example, the Better Business Blueprint (my most popular size) comes in at around 15,000 words and is pocket-sized. It only takes six months from signing the contract to you holding the finished, *published* book in your hands!

3. You'll work with a responsive, collaborative team of professionals.

In traditional and hybrid publishing, it's often hard to get in touch with people who are working on your book. They are busy, busy, busy! Often, they move on to other roles or publishers within a few years, leaving you high and dry.

By contrast, *you'll be working directly with me for the majority of your project.* You'll work closely with me and your ghostwriter for the crafting and writing portion of the project, and with my trusted publishing coordinator to ensure your retail accounts are in order. In addition, my team responds to messages quickly. And more importantly, we are lots of fun to work with! We love what we do and consider it an honor to work on each client's book.

4. I have *actual, real-world* experience with book strategy and marketing.

It is rare to find people in any publishing company who have written, published, and marketed dozens of their own books—and built multiple seven-figure income streams from those books. But that's what you get when you work with me.

I bring a wealth of firsthand experience to each project. This is my sixty-seventh book (and the only one I've had ghostwritten—the rest have been written, every word, by yours truly), and I've sold just shy of five million copies as of this writing, with translations in forty languages.

In addition, I've built more than a dozen six- and seven-figure income streams from those books, including a mastermind, courses, companion guides, coaching, consulting, and more.

In short, I know how to craft, publish, market, and monetize books. It's my passion and my superpower. Not to wax too emotional, but suffice it to say *I love it* and consider publishing books a huge piece of my life's work and legacy.

One more important point: no one will love your book as much as you do, other than me. You won't find that level of commitment, focus, and care through any other publishing option. Period.

5. You work directly with me to strategize, monetize, and publish your book.

My team is intentionally small, and I don't outsource the strategy to anyone else. When you work with me, you get my personal time, attention, and expertise. I work closely with each member of the team on your behalf to ensure your book makes you happy—and lots of money.

That return on your investment is high on my focus list for each book I produce, and I spend concentrated research time to determine the correct direction of the book, applications for the book, the proper metadata, and so much more. All of this goes to determining how to get your book in the hands of readers and prospective clients.

6. We only work with a few select clients at a time.

Larger publishers are very often launching several books per week. Their marketing teams are overwhelmed. It's very common to hear author horror stories of how they felt left out in the cold after their book was released.

When we work together, you get the full attention of a responsive, dedicated team that is here to craft an amazing bespoke book for you. We're always here to answer your questions, and we look forward to staying in touch post-launch!

7. We focus on metrics that actually matter.

Look, I don't have anything against people wanting a bestselling book. But publishing insiders know that bestseller lists are mostly meaningless. They're certainly no indication of quality or profitability for the author.

I prefer to focus on creating a ***best earning book*** for you by being intentional with your monetization strategy. There is zero focus on vanity metrics—you want a ten-times multiple on your investment, year-over-year, and that's my personal goal for you and your book.

There is often an inverse relationship between the size of the publisher and the results they can help you get. We aren't the biggest publishing option, but we do help our clients to get big results!

Now that you've seen how we're different, let's take a look at three different options we currently offer for bespoke books.

Whoever said 'jack of all trades, master of none' never met Honorée Corder. She possesses an extraordinary level of mastery in all aspects of writing, publishing, and book promotion. In fact, my decision to partner with Honorée on The Miracle Morning Book Series *has been one of the best (and most profitable) decisions I've ever made. If you want your book to not only become a bestseller but also make a life-changing impact on your readers and generate significant income for you and your family, there is no one better to work with than Honorée Corder.*

~Hal Elrod, *The Miracle Morning* and *The Miracle Equation*

CHAPTER SEVEN

BESPOKE BOOK OPTIONS

SO FAR WE'VE covered:

- The professionals who strategize, write, edit, design, and publish your book.

- The unique and in-depth process used to create your book.

- Why my process stands apart from other publishing options.

If you're curious about the details, I've got you covered! In this chapter, I've broken down the available options for your book. I'll conclude with some thoughts about how to choose the most effective bespoke book size for you, before we head into Part 3.

TAILORED SOLUTIONS FOR EVERY VISION

As you consider investing in your legacy with a bespoke book, here are the options we currently have available:

MINI MASTERPIECE

- 4×7" design
- Approximately 60 pages of concentrated wisdom (5,000 words)
- Investment range: $25,000 to $40,000

THE BETTER BUSINESS BLUEPRINT

- 4×7" design
- Approximately 120 to 150 pages of impact and insights (15,000 to 30,000 words)
- Investment range: $75,000 to $125,000

THE DEFINITIVE AUTHORITY

- 5×8" or 6×9" format
- Around 150 to 200 pages of comprehensive expertise (45,000 to 70,000+ words)
- Starting investment: $150,000

The best way to think about these options is to keep in mind that your book is a **custom revenue-generating business asset.** Expect to invest approximately $5 to $7 per word for your bespoke publication.

Each all-encompassing package delivers a polished, published book (in e-book and paperback format) meticulously crafted from conception to completion. There are also two publishing add-ons we can discuss: hardcover and audiobook formats may be available for your title. Multiple formats help give the appearance of a traditional publisher and build up your perceived authority. It's not just your book—it's a powerful business asset designed to generate returns for a decade or more.

As a business leader, time is your most valuable resource. Our streamlined process respects your busy schedule.

Most of our authors invest less than twenty hours total in their book's creation. We handle every detail, allowing you to focus on what truly matters: growing your business and savoring your personal time.

WHICH SIZE IS RIGHT FOR YOU?

Earlier in the book I talked at length about the need for your book to have a specific job. When you know what that job is, choosing the right size becomes much easier.

That said, our most popular size is The Better Business Blueprint, which features approximately 120 pages of content in a pocket-sized 4×7" design. (This book's size, in fact.)

We live in an age where most people want the biggest return for their time—especially business leaders who have a lot on their plates. I love books of all sizes, just as long as they are *great*.

But I've noticed an undeniable pattern of people getting genuinely excited about the idea of their prospects reading their short book quickly and almost immediately taking action on what they've read—i.e., going from prospect to client *fast*.

I've seen how our clients' readers have responded to books of this length. They move from "I don't know you, I don't like you, and I don't trust you" to "I know you, I like you, I trust you ... and I want to hire you" quickly.

It doesn't take someone very long to read a short book, so they can experience this transformation from stranger to client in just a few hours (of their time, not yours!).

Sometimes a longer book is more appropriate, though. As of this writing, my team is working on a full-length client book that is a blend of teaching life lessons and memoir. The subject matter is rich, and so the final word count will be around

70,000 words; it was the only size that would do this client's story justice.

Every decision relies on the answer to the question, *What is the job of this book?*

In other words, how much information must be included in the book for the reader to go on that Hero's Journey Kent mentioned, to experience that transformation, to feel that they can finally solve their problem now that they've come to know you through your book?

And what is the job of the book for you, the author? What do you want the reader to do at the end of the book once they've read it?

In our book strategy process, we dig into all of this, so you don't have to figure out any of it on your own. After consulting with you, we'll help you determine the right length book for your mission.

And here's another area you don't have to figure out by yourself: how to maximize your book's impact through publishing and promotion. That's the topic of Part 3, where we're heading next.

— PART THREE —

MAXIMIZING YOUR IMPACT

CHAPTER EIGHT

PUBLICATION OPTIONS AND DISTRIBUTION CHANNELS

NOW THAT YOU have a clear idea about *how* your masterpiece—i.e., your bespoke book—will be created, you're probably wondering *where* it will be made available.

As an author who's written dozens of books, I can tell you that one of the greatest feelings in the world is holding your completed book in your hands and seeing it available to order!

That's where publishing comes in. If appropriate, we will publish your book with several major platforms so virtually anyone in the world can buy (or borrow!) it.

Another option is to create a legacy book, and in these instances, we'll print just a few stunning copies for you to gift to your family and heirs.

Let's dive into your options.

WHERE WILL YOUR BOOK BE PUBLISHED?

Where your book should be published is based on the job of the book. Publishing on all available distribution channels will give you, literally, global distribution. If your book's ideal reader lives far and wide, they'll have the ability to discover your book—and you!

For Phil Hellmuth's *#POSITIVITY*, global distribution made sense, as his fan base inhabits the four corners of the earth.

For the third edition of *American Dream Women* by the mother-daughter team of Mary Lynn Seebeck and Ellen Seebeck Rheinlaender, distribution primarily in the United States made sense.

In some instances, publishing the book by printing copies that are not available anywhere books are sold is the right play. Some authors don't want to sell their books; they simply use their books to market their businesses. Prospective customers cannot buy copies, but they can have as many as they'd like—because the upside for the author and their business is that good!

It's beneficial to apply intentional forethought to every book's distribution to ensure it connects with the intended readers.

WILL YOUR BOOK BE AVAILABLE IN BOOKSTORES?

A common question many clients ask is whether their books will be available in traditional bookstores like Barnes & Noble.

The short answer is *yes*.

It's important to realize that there is no barrier to entry for independent and self-published authors now. Your book can be sold everywhere because it will have access to the same distribution channels traditional publishers use.

For example, traditional publishers distribute through IngramSpark, which makes books available to bookstores. As an independent author you can do the same thing.

It doesn't mean you will walk into any bookstore and your book will be on the shelf. But it does mean that your book will be available for them to stock and for readers to special order. In most instances, you can visit a bookstore and ask them to order your book to have available and they will (especially if you are a local author or are traveling to host a book signing).

However, if having your book on the shelf in a brick-and-mortar store is important to you, then your book marketing plan will include steps to help get your book into bookstores.

AUTHOR COPIES

In addition to seeing your book on all the major platforms for readers, you also have access to *author copies*. These are print copies you can purchase at a *fixed*, low, per-book cost through Amazon, IngramSpark, or printing companies.

The cost is determined by the dimensions and page count, plus paperback or hardcover. Author copies can range between $2.50 and $10, plus tax and shipping.

You have the option to purchase larger quantities for lower per-book prices through printing companies that specialize in printing books. The more you buy, the lower your per-book price.

You can either give these author copies away to prospective clients or sell them at speaking engagements, on your website, or through other channels.

Back in the old days of publishing (and by "old days" I mean up until the early 2000s), it was much more complicated to get author copies. Most of the time, you had to resort to buying thousands of copies from a printing company and storing them in your garage.

It's much more convenient these days. You can log in to your Amazon or IngramSpark account, order as many copies as you need, or order copies through a book printer (the minimum quantity is usually one hundred), and they'll arrive at your doorstep in a few days. As part of our work together, we'll discuss the most effective option for you.

You won't have this same opportunity from a traditional or hybrid publisher. They normally provide a 50 percent author discount (off the retail price), which is quite high compared with the steep discount on author copies you get when you self-publish. As I mentioned earlier, as the owner of your publishing company, you maintain control and ownership of your title and you will have access to this benefit when you publish with me.

As you can see, the preexisting hurdle of distribution for self-published books is gone, and your book can enjoy the same distribution as its fellow traditionally published titles. For more good news, let's continue our conversation by talking about potential marketing strategies.

CHAPTER NINE

MARKETING AND MONETIZING YOUR BESPOKE BOOK

MOST AUTHORS CAN agree about one thing: they hate marketing (or at least the idea of it).

Anytime you use the word "hate" to describe something, that's pretty strong language! But maybe it's appropriate because while most authors love the act of creating their book, they resist the idea of putting themselves out there and promoting their book.

The topic of marketing (and promotion) for authors is a huge topic. So big, in fact, that I've written an entire book about it: *You Must Market Your Book*. I've also created multiple courses, been a guest on countless podcasts, and had thousands of conversations with authors about book marketing.

I can boil it all down to a concept that's very simple; however, especially in relation to a bespoke book that's created for you: we can make an amazing book, but the most important factor in your book's success is still *you*.

Your consistent marketing activities, not to mention your excitement about your book, will make your book the success it's destined to be.

I can tell you what to do, but it will be up to you to make it happen. This is your book, your legacy, and your asset to leverage.

When you put in the work, the book will do its part to bring new business to your door. A lot of authors stunt their business growth because their book isn't out there doing its job: generating new business.

Let me explain further.

A BOOK IN MOTION IS MONEY IN MOTION

I'll say this as directly as I can: your book won't generate business for you unless your book is in circulation. There's a saying I often use with my clients:

A book is money in motion.
A book at rest is money at rest.

If you go to the trouble and expense of creating a book, but you don't spend time promoting and marketing it, the results will not be what you hoped for.

Said another way, there's no mystical force involved, no lightning strike, and no magic bullet. If you're not concentrating on getting your book in motion, it won't meet its potential … and you won't meet yours.

This means getting your book into the hands of strategic partners and prospective clients. It means following up and continuing to do what you've been doing to grow your business.

The difference, though, is that now you're elevated as a brand, as an authority.

The more you get your book into motion, the more it will come back to you. A book is like a boomerang for your business. Maybe now is a good time to invent a new term: the *bookarang*!

People will probably throw your business card away, but they will *never* throw your book away (unless it is of poor quality). They might not read it, but chances are high they'll either pass it on to someone they think would benefit from reading it, or it will be donated. Either way, it's still out there, ready for the right person to read it.

That's why I spend hours, in addition to perfecting your book, on your Book Marketing Action Plan (Book MAP).

YOUR BOOK MAP

Marketing is vital to a book's success. Most authors ignore it, and most publishers (and publishing services) don't understand it, do it very well, or, frankly, have any real-world experience being successful at it.

While they may have produced and published dozens or even hundreds of books, most of these "professionals" haven't written dozens of books, nor have they sold hundreds of thousands, let alone millions, of copies.

If one or several of their authors has achieved this kind of success, they'd be hard-pressed to explain how it happened, or be able to share a process others could follow to replicate that success with their own books.

One of the benefits of working with me on your book is that I understand how to turn books into impact *and* income.

The value of working with a seasoned publishing strategist who has sold millions of books (as opposed to a random book marketing "expert" who knows some tricks but doesn't have firsthand experience) is in the results you'll get once your book is out in the world.

The additional marketing assets I present to you are custom to your book, your business, and your goals (among a few other criteria). You'll receive step-by-step instructions, templates, and even website copy. I haven't found any other publishing service that offers the breadth and depth of tools to their authors that I do. (They don't even know what they are or that they exist!)

Plus, these assets are, again, custom to you and your book—because they are crafted by me after I have come to understand you and your business through our conversations and my extensive reviews of your book.

When I create your Book MAP, I not only focus on getting your book into the hands of readers, I also help you do so strategically. In addition, I provide insight and ideas about the kinds of other higher-ticket offerings your readers might enjoy.

Helping clients dream about how their book can create *big business* (read: an empire!) is truly one of the most exciting parts of the bespoke book process!

YOUR BOOK IS A CATALYST FOR ADDITIONAL PRODUCTS AND SERVICES

Earlier in the book, I talked about the idea that your book is a *catalyst* for your business growth, as well as for your reader as they grow and learn.

One of the coolest parts of getting to dream about the possibilities with my clients is thinking about the various products and services their books might make possible.

In fact, the very act of working with a team that is strategizing, writing, and publishing your book brings up lots of creative possibilities. A common strategy is to repurpose your book's content into other products, such as a workbook, journal, or course.

In addition, you can adapt and expand the material into a workshop, keynote speech, consulting framework, or coaching program.

There are several ways the content of your book can be repurposed. Many times, an author has an idea of what they want to create, but no one has shown them all the possibilities or provided a roadmap. They are under the impression that they just need to have a book—nothing more, nothing less—and that the book exists just to check a box on their résumé.

As a result, most authors don't do much pre-planning for their book. They don't put a lot of thought and intention into the process because they're not thinking about it from a 30,000-foot view. They don't—can't—see the big picture.

I can do that because I've done it, and I'm still living it right now.

A well-crafted, purposeful book can have a radical impact on your reputation, your business—and most importantly, your bottom line!

The vast majority of publishers don't think this way. They publish a book and hope for the best.

But hope is not a book marketing strategy!

When you work with me and my team, you get the invaluable benefit of my experience in marketing your business with your book in addition to repurposing the book's content into many different profitable formats and offerings.

We've come so far on our journey together! In our final chapter, I'll offer you a challenge to take everything you've learned so far and put it into practice.

If you want to be more successful, fulfilled, and prosperous, a bespoke book is one of the best pathways to get there.

CHAPTER TEN

YOUR PATHWAY TO PROSPERITY

I HOPE YOU begin this final chapter filled with a sense of hopefulness and excitement about what a bespoke book can do for you and your business.

I've done my best to help you gain clarity about what's possible with a bespoke book, walk you through the process, and show you ways to maximize your impact with a book. I also hope you now understand why working with me will make a huge difference in every aspect of your future book.

Before issuing a final challenge, it will be helpful to consider a topic many people ask me about: the ROI of a bespoke book. How do you determine if it's worth the investment?

DETERMINING YOUR RETURN ON INVESTMENT

As I've mentioned, we start thinking about your return on investment before we plan your book or even write a word of it. I help you start to think about the ROI from our very first conversation. It's baked into the process from the start. It makes no sense to put the huge effort it takes into creating a book only to find out you've written the wrong book for your purposes. I'm here to make sure your book is in alignment with your vision, purpose, and passion.

This is one of the many things that sets this process apart. It's rare to work with any type of publisher—whether traditional, hybrid, or otherwise—who thinks about how to get a great return on your investment from the very beginning.

For example, we might talk about selling books in bulk or white labeling them so you can sell them to a specific company or organization. Or we might discuss getting your author copies before publishing so you can distribute them and begin generating new business before the official publication date.

There are many, many strategies we can discuss for monetizing your book. Unlike traditional or hybrid publishers, we have those conversations before we outline and write the book.

Why? So those strategies are included in the book itself.

If you are taking a vacation, you don't just get in the car and start driving. You plan your destination from the very beginning—including how you'll get there, the costs involved, where you'll stay, what you'll wear considering the weather, the kinds of activities you'll participate in, and even how long you'll be gone. (And who is going to take care of the dogs?)

Most authors and publishers take the opposite approach with their books. When the book is published, they ask, "Well, what now? Guess it's time to think about a marketing plan!" Or worse, they just sit there and hope their customers will notice it.

By then, it's far, far too late. The book is already out in the world, and missed opportunities (more *opportunity costs*) abound.

Let's look at a little math to help you maximize the ROI of your book. I like to use the metric of *lifetime client value.*

For example, one of my clients is a wealth manager who makes about $180,000 *per year* from just one of his large investment clients. He invested about a third of that with me for his book, so, in order to triple his money, he just needs one client to reach a net positive of $120,000. The rest of the new business generated from his bespoke book is pure profit.

Let's use another example. I have a friend who sells a $15,000 course. When she engages five new clients, for a gross of $75,000, she will have broken even on her investment. Every new client beyond that initial five puts her further and further in the black—every new business opportunity and client resulting from the book after that is gravy.

In 2017, I published a book for a client who still uses the book to generate new business—as of the writing of this book, he has generated over $23 million in new business. He is so happy; he refers to the amount he paid me as a "rounding error." (And it's also his nickname for me.)

This is why doing a bespoke book with me is an *investment*, not an expense.

If you can use your book to make multiple times the investment, or even millions of dollars, consider the investment in your book as part of your marketing budget.

What's even better is that once you have recouped your investment, you have a revenue-generating business asset *forever*. It doesn't expire.

And here's the real kicker: if you're in the services business (such as speaking, coaching, or consulting), you can immediately raise your rates. Why? Because now *you're an author* who is therefore more credible and considered the authority.

This is exactly why speakers command higher fees when they've authored a book. But the math applies to others as well.

If you were charging $15,000 for your coaching program before, once you've released your book you can charge $25,000. You've just given yourself a $10,000 raise.

If you're a consultant, you can increase your fees by 10, 25 or even 50 percent—just by having a book to hand out.

When you become an author with a bespoke book, not only will you be able to charge more for your time, you will get those engagements more often. And once you recoup your initial investment, you will be in the black forever because a great book will continue generating income forever.

THE TRUE VALUE OF BESPOKE BOOK PUBLISHING

When it comes to the return on investment for a professionally published book, the answer isn't simple—it's *extraordinary*.

Imagine a book that doesn't just sit on shelves but actively works for you by:

- Forging powerful author-reader connections
- Opening doors to lucrative opportunities
- Maximizing your monetization potential

When you work with me to professionally publish your book, the real magic happens beyond royalties. Your book becomes a catalyst for attracting high-value clients, commanding premium fees, and establishing unshakeable industry authority.

My process ensures:

- Zero wasted minutes on writing, publishing, or marketing logistics

- A stunning, timely publication
- A bespoke strategy tailored to your personality, schedule, and resources

When you invest in our expertise, you will watch as the idea of a book that you've had for years transforms through a streamlined path to success into the book of your dreams. You'll save countless hours and see returns far sooner than going it alone.

Ultimately, you don't just want to publish a book. The true intention I hold for my clients is to launch a book that is a powerful extension of their brand, and that your new asset will work tirelessly to help you build your empire. As you might imagine, I am only human, and my commitment to excellence limits the number of people I can help. I will only commit to helping you if I can offer you the fullness of the Honorée experience.

Ali Hemyari, whom I mentioned in an earlier chapter, is the owner and founder of Nashville K-9 and Hemyari Family Companies. Together, we published

Discipline: What It Really Takes to Build a Seven-Figure Business. Here's what he had to say about working with us:

"As a successful business owner, I didn't have time to research, write, and publish my book on my own. In fact, my time was better spent working on my business and hiring Honorée to avoid the pitfalls of self-publishing.

"I'm so grateful for Honorée's expert guidance and help. She and her team knocked it out of the park! Now I have a book that perfectly captures my thoughts and voice and will promote my business for years to come."

And, Matt Feret had these kind words about his experience:

"Collaborating with this remarkable publishing team was like discovering hidden treasure. They didn't merely meet my expectations; they obliterated them! Their unwavering dedication, lightning-fast responsiveness, and unwavering support were nothing short of extraordinary. The result? Two meticulously crafted books that accomplish my goal of helping people and driving interaction. If you're contemplating penning your own opus, look no further. This team isn't just about ink and paper; they're architects of enduring relationships. They transformed my publishing journey into a delightful escapade. So, fellow authors, if you've got a book simmering in your soul, trust me—this is the team that will help you weave your story into the fabric of eternity."

Thanks, Ali and Matt!

I want the same experience for you! The question is, where do you go from here?

THE NEXT STEPS ON YOUR AUTHOR JOURNEY

Are you ready to turn your expertise into a book that sells and pays dividends for years to come?

Let's get your valuable insights into the form of a book sooner rather than later. If you're ready to transform your knowledge into a powerful, published book that will work 24/7 for your business for years to come, let's talk.

I'd love to have a candid conversation about your unique goals and how we can align your book to achieve them. If I think we're a good fit, I'll say so. If I don't think we're a good fit, I'll definitely say that.

The true value of authorship is immeasurable—it's a game-changer that elevates your entire professional trajectory.

Here's how the process works:

1. Email me directly at honoree@honoreecorder.com.

2. We'll schedule a personalized consultation via phone or Zoom (or in person if distance allows).

3. I'll ask questions to learn about your book project ideas.

4. I'll answer all of your questions before we engage.

Remember, this isn't just about publishing a book. It's about creating a game-changing, revenue-generating business asset. Our conversation could be the pivotal moment that helps propel your business to new heights and amplifies your influence.

The opportunity to share your wisdom with the world is waiting. *Seize it now.*

Contact me today, and let's start writing your success story. I'm excited to hear about your vision and show you how we can bring it to life.

GRATITUDE

BYRON, THANK YOU for being my husband, best friend, sounding board, supporter, and "all the things." I couldn't do what I do without you.

Renee, you're just the best!

Jizelle and Tim, IFLY!

Kent, your contributions as the writer have been invaluable. Our discussions greatly enhanced the process, and your expertise was essential to this book's success. Thank you for your dedication. Here's to the future!

Dino, Alyssa, and Mike, a great book is only as good as the team who works tirelessly on it. Thank you for *everything* you did for this book, and all of the books we touch.

My bespoke book clients, thank you for entrusting me with your book. No one loves your book more than you do, *other than me*. I appreciate your trust in our work together, and now in our friendship. Here's to more impact!

ABOUT
HONORÉE CORDER

HONORÉE CORDER IS a prolific author with more than sixty-five books (including *You Must Write a Book* and *Write Your First Nonfiction Book*) with almost five million sold worldwide. She's an empire builder with more than a dozen six- and seven-figure income streams and the host of the Empire Builders Mastermind, plus she's a TEDx speaker. Honorée passionately mentors aspiring empire builders, coaching them to write, publish and monetize their books, create a platform, and develop multiple streams of income. Find out more at HonoreeCorder.com or by sending an email to Honoree@HonoreeCorder.com.

Made in the USA
Monee, IL
12 December 2024